MW00946436

Mastering the Art of Scale Aircraft Cockpit Detailing

By Chris "The RC Geek" Wolfe

Here's to the endless possibilities within each build! May this book spark creativity and fuel your passion for scale modeling, empowering you to transform the ordinary into extraordinary.

Table of Contents

Elevating Your Model's Cockpit to New Heights   3

Chapter 1: Introduction to Cockpit Customization   4

Chapter 2: Materials and Tools for Cockpit Detailing   6

Chapter 3: Basic Interior Enhancement   12

Chapter 4: Custom 3D Printing, Decals, and Lighting   18

Chapter 5: Pilot Detailing, Painting and Animation   31

Chapter 6: Case Studies in Scale Cockpit Customization   37

Chapter 7: Embracing the Journey   43

Bonus: Creating Unique Cockpit Details with Everyday Materials   45

Elevating Your Model's Cockpit to New Heights

Welcome to your next step in the journey of scale modeling mastery!

I am Chris "The RC Geek" Wolfe, a passionate advocate for all things aviation and scale modeling. As a two-time RC Scale National Champion at the US Scale Masters (2016 and 2019), my life has revolved around bringing the thrill of flight into the detailed world of RC aircraft. This passion was sparked in the vibrant atmosphere of my father's hobby shop, Jet Hangar Hobbies, Inc., and it continues to drive my desire to share this craft with you through this book.

In "Mastering the Art of Scale Aircraft Cockpit Detailing" we deep dive into the heart of your aircraft models—the cockpit. As such, this book aims to inspire you with detailed techniques and creative insights that I hope will transform your approach to cockpit customization.

In this book, we will explore a comprehensive range of detailing methods, from basic enhancements to advanced digital crafting with 3D printing, designed to elevate the realism and intricacy of your aircraft projects. Each section is crafted to help empower you to take your detailing skills from straightforward modifications to complex, show-stopping interiors.

For additional learning and to further your skills, I encourage you to visit members.thercgeek.com for exclusive video courses, step-by-step tutorials, and personal coaching sessions. Check out thercgeek.com/FinishingResources for a comprehensive guide to the specific tools and materials referenced here. To stay connected with the latest tips, updates, and scale upgrade products, my main website, www.thercgeek.com, is always here to help enrich your modeling experience.

Join me as we delve into the meticulous world of cockpit detailing. Together, we'll transform standard cockpits into extraordinary focal points of your models. Let's gear up and get ready to enhance the heart of your scale aircraft!

Let's get started, and I'm excited to see where your creativity takes you!

Chris "The RC Geek" Wolfe

Guiding your detailed exploration into scale aircraft cockpit artistry

This scratch-built EDF F4D Skyray also features a scratch-built cockpit accomplished using both 3D printed & traditional materials

Chapter 1: Introduction to Cockpit Customization

In RC scale modeling, the magic truly lies in the details. One of the often-overlooked aspects that can completely transform a model from good to great is the attention paid to the cockpit. The cockpit is often the centerpiece of any scale model aircraft and offers a unique opportunity to showcase and develop craftsmanship skills that can be applied not just to the interior but elsewhere too. The reality is that it doesn't take much to transform an otherwise ordinary cockpit. It's surprising what just a few small accoutrements can do inside the interior as even just a lightly detailed cockpit contributes significantly to the overall realism of a model. So, let's dive into the transformative art of cockpit customization, setting the stage for the intricate work that can make your RC scale model a standout piece both on the ground and in the air.

This Freewing F-14 has a fully custom 3D Printed cockpit and moving pilots.

Understanding the Scope of Cockpit Customization

Cockpit customization encompasses a range of modifications from simple additions like changing to more scale pilot figures and basic instrument panels to complex, fully functional dashboards with lights and moving parts. The intention of this book is to discuss the various levels of detailing you can achieve while providing tailored tips & tricks to help with the execution of it all.

- **Basic Detailing:** This includes adding pilot figures, seat belts, and simple instrument panel parts and/or decals. It's a great starting point and can be accomplished with minimal tools and materials.
- **Intermediate Detailing:** Moving beyond the basics, this is where you can start to incorporate more detailed elements such as custom decals, enhanced textures, and more realistic looking items (ejection seats, gauges, etc.).
- **Advanced Detailing:** For those seeking the pinnacle of realism, advanced detailing can involve fully scratch-built instrument panels, incorporating lighting, and adding miniature switches and wires that mimic the complexity of a real cockpit.

Ultimately, the scope of detail is driven by the overall goal for the project and may encompass a combination from the different levels. In most cases, just adding some basic detail with a nicely painted pilot will do wonders for enhancing the realism of an RC scale model.

The Role of 3D Printing

The advent of 3D printing technology has revolutionized many aspects of scale modeling, especially in crafting detailed pilots and cockpits. With the ability to produce precise, customizable components, 3D printing allows modelers to achieve unprecedented levels of detail and accuracy in their cockpit designs that used to require significant time scratch building. Whether it's creating intricate instrument panels, realistic seat textures, or control levers, 3D printing offers a flexible and efficient solution to enhancing cockpit realism. Ultimately the limitation becomes what you can create a 3D model of. However, it is important to consider that the 3D modeling time required to make fine details can be substantial, so you may find that it's quicker to simply carve something from balsawood or foam to build what you need.

Setting Realistic Goals

As we dive deeper into the topic of cockpit customization, it's important to set realistic goals and set aside the appropriate time to achieve those goals. Starting with manageable projects and gradually building up to more complex modifications can help maintain your enthusiasm and prevent feelings of overwhelm. Customizing cockpits is a rewarding aspect of the hobby that enhances not only the aesthetic appeal of your models but also your skill set and satisfaction with your project.

This journey through the art of cockpit detailing is more than just about enhancing aesthetics —it's about embracing passion and patience in scale modeling. Let's embark on this detailed exploration together, transforming standard models into extraordinary showcases of history and craftsmanship.

The detailed cockpit in this refinished F-14 Tomcat contributes significantly to the realism displayed on the ground and in flight.

Chapter 2: Materials and Tools for Cockpit Detailing

Before we get into the detailing side of things, it's important to discuss the essential components and materials pivotal for crafting detailed cockpits for our scale modes. We will explore a diverse range of materials, each integral to the modeler's toolkit and chosen for their particular properties that align with the unique demands of scale modeling. From standard modeling materials such as wood and foam to advanced 3D printed parts, each material discussed offers distinct advantages, depending on the level of detail and functionality required in the cockpit design. Understanding the characteristics of these materials will equip you with the knowledge to select the most appropriate options for your projects, ensuring durability, aesthetic authenticity, and ease of handling in your modeling endeavors.

Balsawood & Depron

When all else fails, you can't go wrong with balsawood and/or depron as a building material for cockpits. Balsawood and depron are two materials prized for their light weight and ease of manipulation, making them excellent choices for interiors and are especially helpful for crafting larger components such as the cockpit base/tub. Balsawood is traditionally used for its excellent carving and shaping properties, ideal for bulkier cockpit elements like seat structures and side panels. depron, a type of foam, offers a fantastic solution for lightweight, larger surface areas that require minimal structural support but maximum visual impact.

Working with these materials involves specific techniques to ensure best results. Cutting should be done with sharp blades to avoid tearing, while adhesive choices should be tailored to the material—CA glue generally suffices for balsawood, whereas foam-safe glues are mandatory for depron to prevent material degradation. Sealing balsawood and depron properly not only enhances durability but also prepares surfaces for a flawless paint finish.The balsawood can be sealed simply by smearing medium CA over the surface followed by a light sanding with 180 grit sandpaper to smooth it out. The depron can be sealed with a few coats of water-based polyurethane such as Minwax Polycrylic.

This F-100 Super Sabre cockpit was built entirely of balsawood with the exception of the pilot which was resin cast. The wood was sealed with CA and then primered and painted.

3D Printed Materials

There's no doubt that 3D printing has opened a whole new frontier in scale modeling, particularly for creating highly detailed and custom-fit cockpit components. Common materials used in 3D printing include PLA, PETG, and ABS for standard filament based printers along with resin for SLA liquid resin printers, each with distinct properties that make them suitable for different aspects of cockpit detailing.

PLA (Polylactic Acid): PLA is favored for its ease of printing and exceptional ability to capture fine details, making it ideal for beginners creating intricate cockpit components. It experiences minimal warping while printing, which helps maintain the precision necessary for detailed parts. However, PLA's low temperature resistance is a significant drawback, as it will deform in hot environments like a sun-exposed cockpit. Additionally, its limited mechanical properties make it less durable and unsuitable for functional parts that undergo stress.

PETG (Polyethylene Terephthalate Glycol): PETG combines increased flexibility and heat resistance, making it suitable for more durable parts that might experience temperature fluctuations. This material is more flexible than PLA, which allows it to absorb impacts without cracking. On the downside, PETG can produce strings or oozing during printing, which requires additional cleanup and is problematic for fine detail parts, and it is also sensitive to UV light, which can degrade the material over time.

ABS (Acrylonitrile Butadiene Styrene): ABS is renowned for its toughness and high-quality finish, offering durability and impact resistance ideal for functional cockpit components. It can be sanded and chemically smoothed to achieve a professional appearance.However, printing with ABS requires a heated bed and high extrusion temperatures and is best done with the printer inside of an enclosure to avoid warping, making it more challenging to work with. It also emits fumes during printing, requiring good ventilation to ensure safety.

SLA (Stereolithography) Resin: Resin is the top choice for ultra-high-detail printing due to its superior resolution and smooth finishes, perfect for tiny gauges and intricate details. The precision of resin is unmatched by filament-based printers, allowing for the creation of exceptionally detailed and smooth components. The major drawbacks include the brittleness of the finished prints, which can crack under pressure, and the need for extensive post-processing, which includes thorough washing with isopropyl alcohol and curing under UV light.

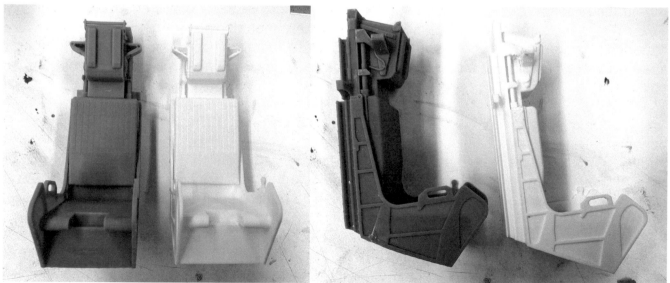

Resin vs Filament Printing: The gray seat on the left was printed out of resin while the white seat on the right was printed out of PETG. Where the resin print shines is in capturing the fine intricate details and surface smoothness.

While no material is perfect, my preferred choice for cockpit detailing will always be resin due to its ability to achieve the smoothest and most detailed finishes. However, filament-based prints, once painted, can also provide excellent results.

Adhesives

Cyanoacrylate (CA) glue is commonly used for its quick setting time and strong bond, making it ideal for most materials including 3D printed plastics and wood. However, for joining heavier or load-bearing components, epoxy provides a stronger bond and longer working time, which can be advantageous for complex assemblies if needed. For materials sensitive to solvents like depron foam, specially formulated foam-safe adhesives are essential to prevent damage during assembly.

Paints and Finishes

The choice of paints and finishes plays a pivotal role in achieving the desired aesthetic of a cockpit project. The selection process involves not only picking the right colors but also understanding the best applications of different types of paints each suited to different detailing tasks. In most cases, my preference is to use enamel paints for brush painting and acrylics for adding depth and detail while leveraging Tamiya AS or TS spray paints wherever possible, especially for the larger parts/surfaces. Additionally, custom mixing colors allows for accurate replication of historical and modern aircraft interiors, especially when the desired color isn't readily available, enhancing the authenticity of the model.

Enamel Paints: For brush painting details within the cockpit, enamel paints are my go-to choice. Enamel paints are valued for their superior adhesion, smooth application, and vibrant color saturation, making them ideal for hand-painted details. Their slower drying time compared to acrylics allows for a smoother finish as the paint has more time to level out, reducing brush strokes visibility. This feature is particularly useful when painting intricate details like instrument panels and side consoles. Brands like Testors and Humbrol offer a wide range of colors that can be thinned and mixed to achieve custom shades, providing the flexibility needed for authentic historical accuracy.

Tamiya AS/TS Spray Paints: When it comes to painting larger areas (tubs, seats, etc.) or needing a uniform coat over complex surfaces, I prefer using Tamiya AS (Aircraft-specific) and TS (general-purpose) spray paints. These spray paints are lacquer-based, offering quick drying times and a tougher finish than acrylics, which is crucial for areas exposed to handling. The AS series is formulated specifically for aircraft models, ensuring that the colors are historically accurate and consistent with real-world aircraft. Using spray paints not only speeds up the process but also ensures a professional-looking finish with an even coat and no brush marks.

Tamiya Clear Paints: For specialized tasks such as coloring HUDs (Heads-Up Displays) and canopies, Tamiya clear paints offer an excellent solution. These paints are available in a variety of clear colors, which are perfect for simulating the tinted or reflective properties of cockpit canopies and HUD elements. For instance, a light coat of Tamiya Clear Blue or Clear Green can mimic the look of reflective glass or electronic displays, adding a layer of realism that enhances the model's fidelity to the actual aircraft. The use of an airbrush is recommended for even and controlled application, preventing the accumulation of paint that can obscure details and ruin the scale effect. Additionally, mixing clear paints with a bit of pearlescent or metallic medium can simulate the shimmering effect seen in some modern HUDs, providing an extra touch of authenticity to your scale model cockpit.

Acrylic Paints/Pigments: Acrylic paints and pigments play a crucial role in the final stages of model detailing, especially for creating washes and adding subtle effects. Their fast-drying time and water solubility (or better yet, Tamiya acrylic thinner) make acrylics exceptionally convenient for applying layers of shading and highlights after the enamel base coat. This flexibility allows for easy adjustments and blending, essential for achieving a realistic weathered look. Acrylic pigments can be diluted with Windex or acrylic mediums to create custom washes that enhance the depth and realism of the model by settling into recesses and highlighting textures. This technique is especially effective for emphasizing the intricate features of pilot figures, cockpit interiors, and other detailed components. Using acrylics for these finishing touches ensures that every detail stands out, contributing significantly to the overall authenticity and visual appeal of the model.

Having a selection of paints & paint brushes is essential for painting an authentic looking pilot & cockpit.

Applying Clear Coats

Applying clear coats is an essential final step in finishing a cockpit, as it seals the paint, adds durability, and applies a common sheen to the surface to match the real-life materials being represented. Whether matte, satin, or gloss, each finish has a significant impact on the visual perception of depth and detail within the cockpit. Ensure that whichever clear coat is used that it is labeled as non-yellowing to keep the colors from tarnishing over time due to UV exposure.

Matte: Reduces glare and is ideal for military or older aircraft to replicate a less reflective surface.

Satin: Offers a soft sheen that mimics semi-gloss materials found in many cockpits, providing a balance between matte and gloss. If you're looking for sheen difference for the instrument panel dials, consider brush painting a satin clear into the dial faces as a last step of the instrument panel finishing.

Gloss: Enhances depth and vibrancy, suitable for newer aircraft or showcasing well-maintained interiors, commercial or private aircraft, etc.
Choosing the right clear coat finish depends on the desired end effect and the historical accuracy of the model. While matte will apply to most projects, there are applications for all sheens as each finish affects how light interacts with the surface details and can significantly impact the perceived depth and realism of the cockpit.

Paint Brushes

Having a selection of paint brush is essential when painting cockpit parts and pilots as you'll find that there's no one perfect paint brush that fills every need. Brushes come in a variety of shapes, sizes, and materials, each suitable for specific tasks. As a bare minimum, I would recommend having 1-2 sizes of detail brushes for painting details and 1-2 sizes of flat brushes for painting larger areas.

Detail Brushes: These small, fine-tipped brushes are essential for painting intricate details such as dials, labels, and switches within the cockpit. Opt for synthetic brushes when using acrylic paints and natural bristles for enamels and oils to achieve the best results.

Flat Brushes: Flat brushes are ideal for applying smooth, even coats on larger surfaces such as instrument panels or side consoles. Their shape allows for precise control of paint application, helping to avoid streaks.

Filbert Brushes: With their rounded edges, filbert brushes are versatile and particularly good for blending and softening edges in painted details, which is beneficial when creating shadow effects or weathering.

Angle Brushes: These brushes are cut at an angle and are excellent for reaching tight corners and for precise line work. They can be particularly useful when painting around protrusions or in recessed areas.

Care and Maintenance of Brushes

Maintaining your brushes is vital to prolong their life and maintain a high quality of finish.Always clean brushes thoroughly after each use, using appropriate cleaners (water for acrylics, mineral spirits for enamels, etc.). Reshape the bristles while wet and allow them to dry horizontally to avoid water seeping into the ferrule, which can loosen the glue and cause bristle loss. Properly cared-for brushes will last a long time and deliver excellent results and make the detailing process more enjoyable.

Using The Right Brushes With The Right Paints

When using brushes with the paints discussed previously, it's important to match the brush type to the paint type. For instance, synthetic brushes are generally better with acrylic paints as they resist swelling and maintain a sharp point. In contrast, natural bristles are perfect for oil-based enamels, as they hold more paint and provide smoother application.Experimenting with different brushes and paints will help you understand the best combinations for your specific project needs.

While you don't need this extensive a collection, having the right paint brushes for the job is essential.

Using Plastic Models and Pictures as Color References

In addition to understanding the properties of various materials and paints used in cockpit customization, it's equally important to choose the right colors to ensure authenticity in your scale models. Plastic models and detailed pictures of actual aircraft provide invaluable references for this purpose.

Learning from Plastic Models: Many modelers (myself included) keep a collection of plastic model kits not only for building but also as a color reference library. These kits come with instructions that include detailed painting guides based on historical data and actual aircraft specifications. By comparing these guides with your projects, you can gain insights into the specific colors used in different eras and for various types of aircraft. This practice helps in achieving a high degree of accuracy in your cockpit color schemes.

Utilizing Photographic References: High-quality photographs of aircraft cockpits, whether sourced from books, museums, or online archives, are crucial for understanding the real-world appearance of cockpit interiors. These pictures capture subtle details not always apparent in plastic models, such as the effects of lighting on color tones and the wear and tear seen in operational aircraft. By studying these photos, you can simulate specific details that add depth and realism to your models. It's also useful to look at multiple sources to cross-verify colors, as lighting and camera settings can alter the appearance of colors in photographs.

A combination of plastic model instructions and full scale photos were used in painting and detailing these A-7 Corsair II cockpit panels.

Transitioning to Practical Application

Having explored the essential materials and tools needed for detailed cockpit customization, we are now equipped with the foundational knowledge to apply these techniques in practical scenarios. In the upcoming chapter, we will delve into basic interior detailing techniques, where you'll learn how to utilize the discussed materials to start transforming your scale model cockpits. From simple enhancements to more complex modifications, we'll illustrate how the right application of skills can bring a cockpit to life, enhancing both the model's realism and your satisfaction as a modeler.

Chapter 3: Basic Interior Enhancements

Beginning with basic detailing techniques is the start of the cockpit transformation process. These foundational skills enhance the aesthetics of your model while also help build the confidence necessary for tackling more intricate customizations later on. Starting simple allows you to develop a keen eye for detail and an understanding of the materials and tools at your disposal. By focusing initially on straightforward modifications, you gradually learn the nuances of scale accuracy and aesthetic fidelity, setting a solid groundwork for advanced projects.

In this chapter, we will cover a variety of basic techniques that are both accessible for beginners and essential for experienced modelers looking to refine their craft. From adding simple yet effective touches like improved pilot figures and detail treatments to an already existing cockpit, each section is designed to guide you through easy enhancements that will dramatically improve the look and feel of your scale model's cockpit. With these skills, you'll be able to transform a stock ARF cockpit into a vivid representation of aviation artistry, providing a satisfying challenge and a rewarding outcome.

Simple Painting to Enhance Stock Cockpits

One of the most effective ways to upgrade the realism of a stock ARF (Almost Ready to Fly) cockpit is through simple painting techniques. Often, these models come with pre-finished parts, which eliminates the need for initial sanding or extensive surface preparation. However, the choice of colors and how they are applied can dramatically transform the basic appearance into something much more convincing and closer to the full scale aircraft. The color choice should closely match the historical accuracy of the aircraft's era, which adds an essential layer of realism. For instance, military aircraft might use specific shades of gray or green, while commercial or civilian aircraft might have more varied or vibrant interiors. Consulting reference materials or authentic photos of the aircraft can guide your color selection.

From there, apply the desired paint colors. Start with a thin base coat, ensuring full coverage without flooding fine details. It's often beneficial to apply multiple light layers rather than a single heavy coat, as this approach builds up a more durable finish and maintains the sharpness of underlying details. Base colors can be painted with spray paints while additional detail colors applied with brush paints. Use a fine brush or an airbrush for a more controlled and even application if needed.

Adding Depth with Shadows and Highlights

Adding depth to your cockpit's detailing can be effectively achieved through the use of shadows and highlights, which play a pivotal role in emphasizing the three-dimensional features and textures of the cockpit interior. This section will guide you through two primary techniques: dry brushing and washes, each designed to highlight different aspects of your cockpit's details.

Dry Brushing Technique

Dry brushing is a painting technique that involves using a dry brush with a small amount of paint to lightly brush over the raised details of the cockpit. This method is excellent for enhancing textures and edges that might otherwise blend into the background. To begin, dip the tip of a dry, stiff-bristled brush into paint, then wipe off most of the paint on a paper towel until the brush is almost dry. Gently sweep the brush over the areas where you want to highlight details and watch the details begin to pop. The key is to use a very light touch to allow the paint to catch only on the highest points, leaving the recessed areas untouched. This creates a natural-looking highlight that accentuates the textures and shapes of the cockpit's features.

For paint colors, simply take the base color used for whichever part being dry brushed, place a small amount onto a 3x5 card, mix a little white with it to lighten and then start the dry brushing process. When doing so, you'll create the illusion of wear along the part as it will collect on corners and similar areas. For paint chipping, silver is the paint of choice.

Experiment with his technique as it's simple to do and you'll find that it can be leveraged extensively to provide an extremely convincing weathered look.

Using Washes for Depth

To deepen the cockpit's details and add shadows, a specific technique involving acrylic washes can be used. For achieving a realistic shadow effect, I recommend using FolkArt Raw Umber, lightly thinned with Windex. This combination allows the wash to flow smoothly into the recessed areas of the cockpit, and around controls, providing a subtle yet impactful shadowing that enhances the model's depth.

Once the wash is applied, allow it to settle into the crevices to outline and define the details. After a brief setting period, clean up any excess wash from the raised surfaces using a paper towel dampened with Tamiya acrylic thinner. This step is crucial as it prevents the wash from clouding the finer details, ensuring that only the recesses retain the wash, thus accentuating the shadows without diminishing the clarity of the overall paintwork. In addition, Tamiya makes a 'panel line accent' product in various colors that can be used to effectively darken sharpen corners and bring out ultrafine details.

Dry brushing is a simple & effective way to add depth to even the most simple of parts.

A combination of mostly dry brushing with some light washes were used in this F-14 cockpit.

By combining dry brushing to highlight raised details and using a targeted wash to deepen shadows, these techniques can significantly contribute to the visual depth and authenticity of the cockpit. The reality is that even just using one of these techniques will dramatically transform the looks of an otherwise uniform looking cockpit.

Enhancing Realism with Minimal Additions

Enhancing the realism of a scale model cockpit does not always require complex or extensive modifications. Sometimes, small additions can make a significant difference in how authentic the model appears. One such effective and simple addition is the use of cardstock or thin sheet styrene plastic to create panel hood shades, which can add depth and sophistication to the cockpit's layout.

In addition, for foam ARF models, using this to cover the foam parts will prevent and/or hide any "gatoring," which is the swelling of foam beads under the paint that can mar the texture and appearance of the cockpit. This covering acts as a smooth base that not only prevents textural anomalies from coming through but also provides a consistent surface for painting. This can be done across the cockpit as a whole (seats, floors, etc.) if the entire assembly is foam.

Cardstock and/or Sheet Styrene Details

Cardstock and sheet styrene plastic are excellent materials for adding simple details or covers for foam or wood parts due to their flexibility, ease of cutting, and the smooth finish it can provide. Start by carefully measuring the areas you want to cover or add detail to use a sharp hobby knife and a straight edge to cut to the desired size, ensuring clean and straight edges. Once cut, the next step is fitting the pieces into the cockpit. Test fit the piece several times and trim as necessary to get a snug fit. This might require several adjustments, but precision here is key to achieving a seamless look. When you're satisfied with the fit, secure the pieces using a suitable adhesive that won't warp or damage the material (spray adhesive for cardstock, CA for styrene).Once in place, everything can be painted and weathered as desired.

These minimal additions, while small in scope, can have a transformative effect on your model, contributing significantly to its overall realism. By using these materials to create detailed elements like panel hoods and or covers for existing parts, carefully finishing them to blend seamlessly with the cockpit, you enhance the depth and authenticity of the model, making it a more visually appealing representation of the full-scale aircraft.

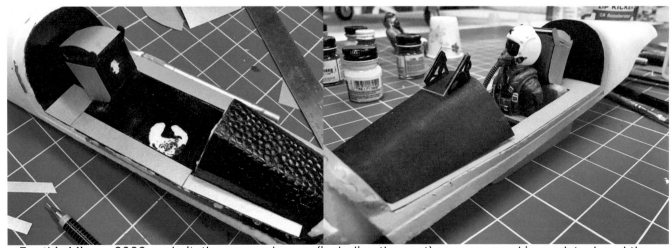

For this Mirage 2000 cockpit, the exposed areas (including the seat) were covered in cardstock and then painted in the proper colors. This hides texture and provides a sheet metal smooth look in the process.

Creating Realistic Seat Belts and/or Canvas Covers with Gaffer's Tape

One simple detail is the addition of seat belts in the cockpit, which not only adds depth to the interior but also increases the authenticity of the model. Gaffer's tape, with its durable fabric-like texture, is an excellent material for simulating realistic-looking seat belts.

Gaffer's tape is a versatile, strong, and easily removable tape commonly used in the film, television, photography, and theater industries. Its primary use is for securing cables to floors, walls, and other surfaces where minimal visibility and safety are essential. The tape's matte finish prevents it from reflecting light, making it ideal for use on set or stage, where it won't be caught by lighting and potentially disrupt the visual scene. Additionally, gaffer's tape is prized for its residue-free removal, meaning it doesn't leave sticky adhesive behind when peeled off, unlike many other tapes like duct tape.

Gaffer's tape has a great canvased look. When painted and weathered, it mimics seat belts and canvas covers beautifully.

With Gaffer's tape in hand, measure and cut the gaffer's tape into strips that will serve as the seat belts. Ensure that the lengths are proportional to the cockpit size and seat dimensions. For added realism, cut the ends of the tape at an angle or curve them slightly to mimic the natural wear and shape of actual seat belts.

Although gaffer's tape comes in various colors, it receives paint very well and so painting is recommend to match specific seat belt colors used in different aircraft or eras. After painting, you can add details such as belt buckles if desired and adjustment hardware using thin wire or small pieces of styrene plastic, painting them metallic to simulate metal.

Affix the prepared seat belts to the cockpit seats using the adhesive on the tape. For a more permanent adhesion, tiny drops of glue can be used. Position them to simulate natural draping and securing points. Ensure that the belts interact realistically with other cockpit elements, such as the seat back and cushions.

To enhance their appearance, apply a light wash or dry brushing over the seat belts to highlight the texture and create shadows that define their contours more clearly. This step brings out the details and makes the seat belts look more integrated into the cockpit environment.

Upgrading with a More Scale Pilot Figure

Upgrading the pilot figure in your scale model cockpit is a straightforward yet impactful way to elevate the overall realism of your aircraft. A well-chosen and skillfully painted pilot figure can become a focal point that draws attention and adds life to the model. While discussed in full detail in Chapter 5 including sources and sizing tips for pilots, this section will guide you through applying some simple painting techniques to maximize realism.

Simple Painting Techniques for Pilot Figures

The first step is to select the right size and style of pilot figure. Start by applying a solid base color to each part of the figure, such as the flight suit, helmet, and accessories. I will usually spray paint the pilot white since the helmets are typically white and then brush on enamel paints for the remaining colors. While most flight suits are green and helmets are white, using resources and pictures can help inform color choices as modern fighter G-suits can have some color variation in the green. Also, pilots customize their helmets to suit their squadrons, so that is something fun to do as well. In all cases, it's important to let each color dry completely before applying adjacent colors to avoid smudging.

After the base colors are applied, enhance the figure's details and textures through dry brushing. This technique involves lightly brushing a lighter shade over the raised details to highlight them. Focus on areas that would naturally catch light, such as the helmet ridges, folds in the flight suit, and facial features, to bring out the depth and texture.

Adding washes is another technique to add additional depth. A wash of a darker shade can be applied into the recesses and crevices of the figure, such as the lines in the flight suit and the edges of the helmet. This process creates shadows and adds a depth that makes the figure appear more lifelike. Be sure to use a small brush and a controlled hand to keep the wash from overwhelming the details. Additionally, it's important to blend the wash color to the base color in the process so that a more natural look and transition in color is apparent.

If you're looking to explore the use of various layers of oil paints to get the most realistic look from the painting process for facial features, there is a fantastic guide specific to pilot figure painting available at acesofiron.com

Many times simply adding a scale pilot can do wonders for enhancing realism of a scale project.

Reflecting on Techniques and Fostering Experimentation

Throughout this chapter, we have explored a variety of fundamental skills—from simple painting enhancements and adding depth with shadows and highlights, to utilizing cardstock and styrene for panel modifications and carefully selecting and detailing a scale pilot figure. Each technique has the potential to significantly improve the visual realism and authenticity of your scale model aircraft and doesn't take a considerable amount of time to accomplish.

Experimentation within these techniques is highly encouraged. The beauty of scale modeling lies in the unique touch each modeler brings to their craft. By experimenting with the methods discussed, such as varying the dry brushing intensity or mixing custom wash colors, you can develop a personalized approach that best suits your style and the specific requirements of your models.

To assess the impact of each modification, take a step back and review your work from a viewer's perspective. Consider taking photos at various stages of the detailing process; this can provide a different viewpoint and highlight areas that may need further enhancement or adjustment. Ask yourself whether the modifications simulate the desired scale accuracy, enhance overall realism, or perhaps even tell a story about the aircraft's operational history.

Furthermore, always be open to identifying additional details that could enrich the cockpit. Does the instrument panel need more defined gauges? Could seatbelts be added? Is the pilot figure painted in line with the aircraft's era and use? These are the types of questions that can guide your decisions and inspire further improvements.

In summary, the techniques outlined in this chapter are just the beginning. Continue to learn, adapt, and innovate, and most importantly, enjoy the creative journey that scale modeling offers.

The basic interior enhancements discussed in this chapter resulted in the cockpit built for this IAI Kfir project that was kit bashed from a Freewing Mirage 2000. Cardstock was used to enhance the stock cockpit and an aftermarket pilot from thercgeek.com/pilots was painted and installed to accomplish the final result.

Chapter 4: Custom 3D Printing, Decals, and Lighting

In the pursuit of unparalleled realism and intricate detail, this chapter invites you to explore the frontier of advanced interior customization. As technology advances and the tools at our disposal become more sophisticated, the potential to create incredible detail to enhance the authenticity and functionality of scale model aircraft cockpits expands dramatically. This chapter is dedicated to integrating cutting-edge techniques and modern innovations that can transform a standard model into a stunningly detailed masterpiece.

By the end of this chapter, you will have a thorough understanding of what is possible so that you may employ these advanced techniques in your modeling projects. The methods presented not only elevate the detail and functionality of your aircraft cockpits but also will undoubtedly set your models apart as exemplars of what can be achieved in the realm of scale modeling. Ultimately, the depth of detail you achieve depends on the time you choose to invest; with today's technology, time becomes the only real limitation since it is now possible to 3D print plastic model quality parts.

Designing and Implementing 3D Printed Parts for Enhanced Detail

3D printing has transformed the landscape of RC scale modeling, offering modelers an extraordinary level of precision and the flexibility to create custom parts tailored specifically to their projects. Understanding the process and what's currently available not only enhances the customization possibilities but also significantly expands the detail and authenticity of your model aircraft interiors.

CAD Design Considerations and Preparation for 3D Printing

The journey to creating custom 3D printed parts begins with a good design, crafted using Computer-Aided Design (CAD) software. This powerful tool allows modelers to build detailed digital models of parts before physically producing them, providing the ability to visualize and tweak designs with unprecedented precision. While this book is not intended as a comprehensive CAD design manual, it's important to grasp the fundamental process and consider key design aspects specific to 3D printing.

There are numerous CAD programs available, ranging from free versions suitable for beginners to more sophisticated, costly software offering more advanced features. If you are new to CAD, starting with free software can be a practical way to gain familiarity without upfront investment. There is a rather steep learning curve initially (though there are some great free learning tutorials on YouTube), but the more your practice and the more CAD models you create, the quicker it gets. As you explore these options, you'll encounter two primary types of CAD systems: parametric modeling and 3D surfacing.

Parametric Modeling: is highly structured, allowing you to create models based on geometric and functional relationships. This type of CAD is ideal for parts that require precise dimensions and engineering specifications, as it lets you easily adjust features and dimensions through parameters which then get reflected through the CAD model as a whole.

3D surfacing: is more flexible and artistic, better suited for creating complex or organic shapes. This method allows for more free-form design but can be less precise when it comes to making adjustments or engineering exact specifications but can be a simpler means of creating fine detail panels, etc.

Both approaches lead to high-quality designs but differ in their design methods and applications. Choosing between them really depends on what you find most useful to you. They both will ultimately result in the same model, it's the workflow getting there that varies.

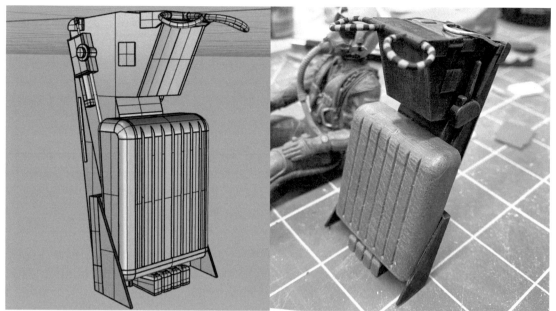

The CAD image of an F-14 Tomcat seatback compared to the final 3D printed and painted part. It requires considerable time to create a finely detailed CAD model.

General CAD Design Process

Creating detailed and accurate 3D printed parts involves a structured design process using (CAD) software. Here's how you can systematically approach the design of custom parts for your model aircraft. As you consider designing your own 3D printed parts, keep in mind that every single detail requires being modeled in the CAD program. In many cases, once a single item is created (e.g a switch), it can be copied around to other areas as needed, but it must be initially modeled first.

Initial Sketching: Start your design process by sketching out your part ideas. This can be done traditionally on paper or directly within the CAD software using digital sketching tools. This preliminary step helps clarify your vision and serves as a visual guide throughout the design process. Sketching allows you to experiment with different concepts quickly and effectively, setting a clear direction before you commit to the detailed design in the CAD environment.

Modeling the Part: With a sketch as your guide, begin modeling the part in your chosen CAD software. In some cases, you may be able to import your sketch or a 2D drawing into the CAD environment to trace over it. Start with basic geometric shapes that form the core structure of your part. Utilizing the tools available in your CAD program, such as extrude, revolve, and loft, you can transform these simple shapes into more complex forms. As you refine your design:

- Extrude to extend a 2D shape into a 3D form.
- Cut and/or Trim to remove material from your model, helping define intricate details or create openings.
- Refine the geometry to smooth edges or add fine details, ensuring that every aspect of the model meets your specifications.

This stage of the process allows for the incremental building of complexity, ensuring that each element of the design is precisely controlled and visually consistent with your initial sketch.

Scaling and Measurement

Accuracy in scaling and measurement is vital to ensure that the 3D printed part fits perfectly within the specified location in your aircraft cockpit. To achieve this:

- Measure dimensions directly from your physical model or obtain detailed measurements from plans or manuals of the actual aircraft.
- Enter these measurements into the CAD software to set the dimensions of your digital model accurately.
- Continuously check the scale as you model, adjusting dimensions as necessary to ensure that the final product will integrate seamlessly with the existing parts of your model.

Consider using a scaling tool within your CAD program to compare the designed part against a scaled outline of your model or a particular section of your model. This practice helps in visualizing how the part will fit into the overall model and is essential for avoiding scale discrepancies between the designed part and the physical model.

Designing for 3D Printing Considerations

When designing parts for 3D printing, several specific considerations must be addressed to ensure that the final print is both feasible and of high quality. These considerations are crucial for avoiding common pitfalls associated with 3D printing such as structural weaknesses, difficulties in post-processing, and issues with assembly fitting. Ultimately as you are designing, it's essential to think about how the printer will be building the part on the 3D printer build plate. Here's a deeper look into some of the critical aspects:

Wall Thickness

The thickness of the walls in your 3D model is a pivotal factor in the success of your print. Walls that are too thin may not print correctly, leading to warping or failure during the printing process. Additionally, thin walls can result in a printed part that is too fragile and prone to breaking under normal handling.

- **Minimum Thickness:** Ensure that every part of your model meets the minimum wall thickness recommended for the printing technology and material you are using. For instance, a typical minimum wall thickness for resin-based printers might be 0.2 mm, but this can vary.
- **Uniformity:** Try to keep wall thickness consistent throughout the model, as varying thicknesses can lead to uneven stress distribution and potential weak spots.

Overhangs and Supports

Overhangs, parts of the design that extend outward beyond a certain angle from the vertical, can be particularly challenging in 3D printing. These require support structures during printing to prevent the material from drooping or collapsing.

- **Design Modifications:** Where possible, design parts to minimize overhangs. This might involve adding fillets, changing the orientation of the part during printing, or designing the part to be assembled from multiple pieces post-printing.
- **Support Strategy:** If supports are necessary, plan for how they will be removed during post-processing. Ensure that supports do not attach to very delicate areas of the model to prevent damage during removal.

Assembly Tolerance

The accuracy of 3D printing isn't perfect, and slight deviations in dimension can occur due to material properties and the specifics of the printing process. When designing parts that will fit together, it's essential to accommodate these potential variations through proper tolerancing (i.e. allowing sufficient extra space for the parts to fit together).

- **Shrinkage and Warping:** Account for the potential shrinkage or warping of materials, especially when using high-temperature materials like ABS. Adjust your designs accordingly to ensure that all parts fit together as intended.
- **Fit Testing:** Design with slight tolerances to ensure parts will fit together without requiring excessive force. For instance, if a pin is designed to fit into a hole, designing the pin 0.1 mm smaller in diameter than the hole might provide a good fit.
- **Material Specifics:** Different materials may require different tolerance strategies. For example, resin might exhibit different shrinkage properties than filament-based materials like PLA or ABS.

By carefully considering these design factors you can significantly enhance the success rate of your 3D printed parts. These considerations not only improve the printability and structural integrity of the parts but also ensure that they function well within the larger context of your scale model project.

Accessing Pre-designed 3D Models

If you're feeling a bit overwhelmed thinking about designing your parts, you're not alone, especially if you've never designed anything in CAD before. Thankfully, another practical avenue to explore is the utilization of pre-designed 3D models. Online platforms such as TheRCGeek.com, Thingiverse.com, Cults3D.com, and MyMiniFactory.com provide extensive libraries of ready-to-print 3D models, which can significantly streamline your project timeline.

These websites are treasure troves of 3D printable models uploaded by a diverse community of designers and enthusiasts. These resources offer a variety of designs that can complement your own creations or in some cases, provide exactly what you are looking for in a complete design for your specific aircraft model. Utilizing these models can not only save you valuable time but also introduce you to different design styles and techniques that might not have been previously considered. Once a suitable model is selected, it can be downloaded typically in STL format, ready to be imported into your slicer software for further adjustment and printing.

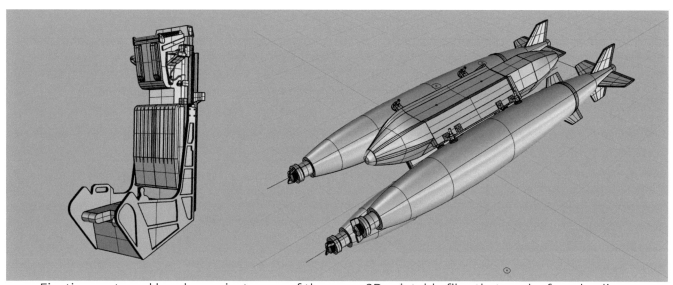

Ejection seats and bombs are just some of the many 3D printable files that can be found online.

Using 3D Printer Slicer Software

Once your part has been designed in a CAD program, or downloaded, the next critical step before printing is to use slicer software. This software plays a pivotal role in 3D printing by converting the 3D CAD model into a format that a 3D printer can understand—specifically, a series of layers that are printed one at a time to create the final part. Here's a detailed walkthrough of how to effectively use slicer software:

Loading the Model: Begin your 3D printing process by importing the model file, typically in STL or OBJ format, into your slicer software. This software acts as a bridge between your 3D model and the 3D printer, translating your design into a language that the printer can understand.

Orientation: Once loaded, carefully adjust the orientation of the model on the virtual print bed. Proper orientation is essential as it significantly impacts the print's duration, the amount of support needed, and the overall quality of the finished part. For example:

- Orient parts to minimize overhangs that require support.
- Position them to maximize the strength along load-bearing axes, enhancing the structural integrity of the printed object.

Placement: Ensure the model is optimally placed within the printable area of the print bed. Adjust its position to optimize material usage and printing time, making sure it is perfectly centered and aligned according to the printer's capabilities.

Slicing Parameters: After setting up the model in the slicer software, you will need to adjust various parameters that directly affect the printing process:

- **Layer Height:** This setting determines the resolution of the print. A smaller layer height results in higher resolution and more detailed prints but increases the printing time.
- **Print Speed:** The speed at which the printer operates can influence the quality of the print. Faster speeds can reduce print time but may compromise layer adhesion and accuracy.
- **Temperature Settings:** Proper temperature settings for both the extruder and the print bed are crucial for achieving optimal print quality. These settings vary depending on the material used and should be adjusted according to the manufacturer's recommendations.
- **Infill Settings:** Decide on the density of the infill structure inside the print. Higher infill density increases the strength of the printed part but also uses more material and extends print time.

Addition of Supports: Identify areas within the model that require support structures to prevent sagging or collapse during the printing process. Slicer software can automatically generate these supports, or you can manually place them for more precise control.
·Configure the supports to ensure they are effective yet easy to remove after printing.
·Consider the density and type of support. Denser supports provide better stability but can be challenging to remove and may damage the print surface.

Simulation: Use the slicer's preview function to simulate the entire printing process. This feature visually demonstrates a layer-by-layer buildup of the model, helping you to anticipate how the printer will construct each section.

Review and Adjust: Carefully review the simulated print path to identify any potential issues, such as unsupported overhangs or areas with excessive or insufficient infill. Make necessary adjustments to the model orientation, support structures, or slicing parameters.

Iteration: It may be necessary to go through several iterations of adjustments and previews to finalize the setup. Each iteration should bring you closer to optimizing print quality and efficiency.

By meticulously setting up your model in slicer software and optimizing the parameters and support structures, you ensure that your 3D printer produces the highest quality parts possible. This preparation is critical for successful 3D printing, especially for complex parts used in scale modeling where detail and structural integrity are paramount.

Filament-Based Printers vs. Resin Printers

When talking about 3D printers, the reality is that filament-based printers are sufficient for most things. However, when talking about extremely fine detail parts, this is where resin printers really shine. Each type (filament-based vs resin) has its strengths and is suited to different aspects of the modeling process.

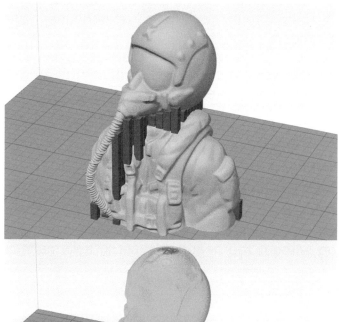

The above pilot model setup for filament printing. The supports are shown in red in the first image with the bottom image showing a preview of the fully sliced model giving a simulation of the final print.

Filament-Based Printers: Known technically as Fused Deposition Modeling (FDM) printers, filament-based printers work by melting a plastic filament and extruding it through a heated nozzle to form the layers of the 3D print. These printers are popular due to their cost-effectiveness and ease of use, making them a great choice for hobbyists and beginners. They can utilize a variety of materials like PLA, ABS, and PETG, each offering unique properties such as durability, flexibility, and different levels of thermal resistance. Generally, these printers are less expensive both in initial setup and material costs. They are quite user-friendly and usually provide a larger build volume, which is ideal for larger models or parts. However, the surface finish of prints from filament printers tends to be rougher with more visible layer lines, often requiring additional sanding and finishing.

Resin Printers: On the other hand, resin printers, which include Stereolithography (SLA) and Digital Light Processing (DLP) technologies, use a liquid resin that hardens when exposed to a specific light source. These printers are renowned for their ability to produce incredibly detailed prints with a much smoother finish than filament-based printers. They are perfect for creating intricate models such as detailed cockpit instruments or pilot figures that

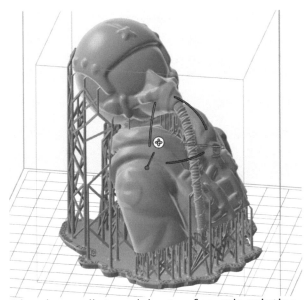

The above pilot model setup for resin printing. Based on how resin printers work, they require different model orientation considerations and supports for 3D printing.

require fine features and a high-quality surface finish. While resin printers operate faster than FDM printers in many scenarios and can produce parts with superior detail, they tend to have smaller build volumes and higher running costs. The materials used in resin printing are more expensive and require careful handling due to their toxicity. Additionally, post-processing is more labor-intensive, involving washing the prints in alcohol and curing them under UV light.

Both types of printers have significant roles to play in scale modeling, each bringing different advantages to the table. By assessing your particular needs in terms of the types of parts you are printing, your budget, and how much time you are willing to dedicate to post-processing, you can make an informed decision that enhances your modeling experience and outcomes.

Both types of printers have significant roles to play in scale modeling, each bringing different advantages to the table. By assessing your particular needs in terms of the types of parts you are printing, your budget, and how much time you are willing to dedicate to post-processing, you can make an informed decision that enhances your modeling experience and outcomes.

Options for Custom 3D Printing Services

If you don't own a 3D printer but still want to take advantage of the unique benefits that 3D printed parts offer for your scale modeling projects, there are several options where you can have your models custom printed. Utilizing these services can be a convenient and cost-effective way to access high-quality 3D printing without the need to invest in and maintain your own equipment.

Options for Custom 3D Printing Services

If you don't own a 3D printer but still want to take advantage of the unique benefits that 3D printed parts offer for your scale modeling projects, there are several options where you can have your models custom printed. Utilizing these services can be a convenient and cost-effective way to access high-quality 3D printing without the need to invest in and maintain your own equipment.

Online 3D Printing Services

If you don't have a 3D printer, or have a filament printer and are looking for resin quality prints, there are many online platforms offer custom 3D printing servicesHere are some steps and considerations for using these services:

The RC Geek: Offers specialized printing services tailored for RC hobbyists, providing expert advice and support specifically in the realm of scale modeling.

Shapeways: Known for its high-quality prints and a broad range of material options.

Sculpteo: Provides fast, reliable service with a wide selection of materials.

i.Materialise: Features intricate design capabilities with numerous finishing options.

By considering these options for custom 3D printing, you can efficiently incorporate complex, precision-made parts into your scale models without needing to own and operate a 3D printer. Whether you choose an online service for its convenience and range of materials or opt for a local provider for the hands-on support, these services can greatly enhance the scope and quality of your modeling projects.

Samples of resin printed pilots and cockpit parts from The RC Geek. 3D printing in resin provides a near plastic model like finish.

Painting and Installing 3D Printed Parts

Once your 3D printed parts are ready, they can be treated much like a plastic model at this point being painted, weathered and prepped for installation into the model. These steps enhance the visual appeal and ensure the parts blend seamlessly with the existing model components. One important note is to dry fit all of the parts prior to painting as you may find that modifications may be necessary for proper fitment.

Painting 3D Printed Parts

Start with thorough surface preparation to ensure the best possible finish. First, clean the parts to remove any residual printing supports or dust. For parts printed from resin, make sure they are washed in isopropyl alcohol and fully cured under UV light (not necessary if received via a third party). Next, sand the parts as needed with fine-grit sandpaper to remove any visible layer lines or surface imperfections being careful not to sand away any of the printed details. This is particularly crucial for filament-based prints.

Apply a primer appropriate for the type of 3D printing material used (Tamiya Plastic Model Primer or Dupli-Color Filler Primer are good options). Primer not only smooths the surface but also enhances paint adhesion. Once the primer is dry, proceed to paint the base coat using an airbrush or spray can for a uniform application. Choose colors that align with your model's scale cockpit scheme.

For detailed painting and additional effects:

• Use fine brushes to apply details such as instrument markings, buttons, and other intricate features using acrylic or enamel paints.

- Integrate weathering techniques to add realism (discussed in the previous chapter).Techniques such as dry brushing can highlight raised details by applying a lighter shade of the base color. Washes can be used to accentuate shadows and depth, applying a darker shade that settles into crevices and enhances texture visibility.

Finally, seal the paintwork with a clear coat to protect it from scratches and handling. Choose a matte, satin, or gloss finish based on the desired look of your model, ensuring it complements the overall aesthetic.

For adhering the parts, select an adhesive that works well with both the printed material and the model's components. Medium Cyanoacrylate (super glue) is typically sufficient for small, non-load-bearing parts, while epoxy might be preferred for heavier or structural components. Apply the adhesive sparingly to prevent overflow, which could mar the appearance. If the positioning requires precision or potential adjustments, opt for a slow-setting adhesive.

Complete the installation with final adjustments such as touch-up painting or additional detailing. Consider adding final weathering touches to integrate the new parts into the existing areas of the model, using any of the previously discussed techniques to convey age and operational wear.

On these 3D printed panels and consoles, the base colors were spray painted and the remaining colors were brush painted. The instruments were accomplished by the use of custom LaserJet printed decals.

Creating and Utilizing Instrument Dial Decals from Source Material

One of the biggest challenges can be creating proper instrument dial faces for use in custom instrument panels and consoles. Using some creative custom decals, we can significantly enhance the realism of scale model cockpits by adding authentic-looking instrumentation without the need for intricate hand-painting. By integrating custom decals into your modeling projects, you not only elevate the level of detail in your creations but also enhance the overall presentation and historical accuracy of the finished piece. This method opens up new possibilities for customization and precision, allowing you to bring a professional touch to your scale models. This section will guide you through the process of creating and applying custom decals for instrument dials, using images sourced from various materials.

Sourcing Accurate Imagery

To begin creating custom decals for your scale model's cockpit, the first step is sourcing accurate images of full scale aircraft instrument panels. These images can be found in a variety of places:

Books and Publications: Aviation books and historical aircraft manuals often contain detailed photographs or diagrams of cockpit layouts. These provide precise references that are invaluable when creating accurate decals.

Online Archives and Museums: Many aviation museums maintain extensive digital collections, including photographs and technical drawings of aircraft. These collections are often accessible online, where some museums also offer 3D cockpit views that provide a comprehensive look at the instrument panels from multiple angles.

Enthusiast Websites and Plastic Model Sites: Websites dedicated to aircraft modeling and aviation history, as well as those catering to plastic model enthusiasts, frequently host galleries of detailed imagery. These sites can be a rich source of photographs and diagrams that are perfect for decal creation.

Internet Searches: Conducting a broad internet search can also yield high-quality images from a variety of sources. Search engines can direct you to images posted in forums, blogs, or news articles which might capture unique or rare views of aircraft cockpits.

When utilizing these images, it is crucial to verify that you have the appropriate rights to use them. Always check the copyright status of each image and, if necessary, obtain permission or a license for personal use. Respecting copyright laws is essential to avoid legal complications and to maintain ethical standards in your modeling projects. By adhering to these guidelines, you can ensure that your source materials are not only useful but also legally and ethically obtained.

Designing Decals

Once you have sourced high-resolution images of aircraft instrument panels, the next essential step in creating custom decals for your scale model involves using graphic design software. This process ensures that the final decals are perfectly scaled and clearly detailed to enhance the realism of your model's cockpit.

Image Preparation: Start by importing your chosen images into a graphics manipulation program, such as Corel Draw (MS PowerPoint works as well). Adjust the scale of these images to match the dimensions of your model's cockpit, which may require precise calculations to ensure that the decals are printed at the exact size needed. Maintaining accurate scale is critical to ensure that the decals fit perfectly within the cockpit's constraints.

Enhancing Clarity: Enhance the clarity of the images by adjusting their brightness, contrast, and sharpness if needed. This step is vital as it ensures that all details are clear and visible, which is particularly important for maintaining readability at the small scale typical of model cockpits.

Decal Layout: Arrange the instrument dials and other cockpit details in a layout that maximizes the use of space on your decal sheet and minimizes waste. Depending on the design of the cockpit panel, especially if it includes holes for instruments, you might opt to layout the instruments exactly as they would appear on the panel. This approach allows you to place the entire sheet behind the panel, simplifying the installation process. Alternatively, you might decide to prepare the designs for individual cutting and placement. In this case, print the designs on white decal paper and meticulously cut each decal to size. For cutting small circle decals, such as dials and gauges, using sharpened brass tubes can be highly effective for achieving clean, precise cuts.

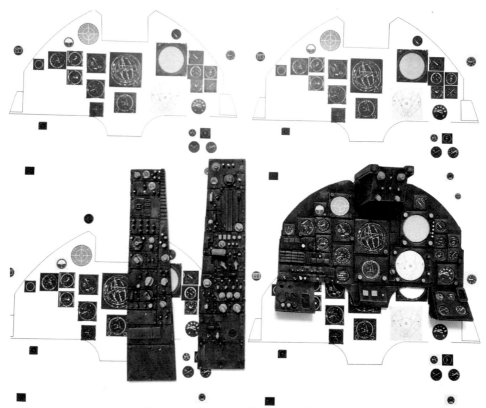

The instrument dials for these A-7 Corsair II panels were created from numerous sources and laid out in the configuration and printed on white decal paper. Each decal was cut using a sharpened brass tube and placed individually.

This methodical approach to designing and preparing decals ensures that when applied, they significantly enhance the authenticity and depth of your scale model's cockpit, providing a level of detail that might otherwise be unachievable through painting alone. It's worth noting that in some cases, you may find a complete instrument panel image which along could be used in the cockpit to create the cockpit panels. While it won't provide much in the way of 3D texture, you may find that it works well enough for your desired project.

Printing and Applying Decals

When it comes to printing custom decals, the type of decal paper and printer you use can significantly affect the quality and durability of the final product. For modelers looking for the best durability and ease of use, using laser decal paper with a laser printer is highly recommended. Laser printers use toner instead of ink, which does not smear and is highly resistant to water and UV light, making it ideal for models that might be exposed to various elements. Additionally, laser decal paper is specifically designed to withstand the high temperatures of laser printing, ensuring that the paper does not melt or warp during the printing process. This combination allows for faster printing without the need for drying time, and the prints themselves are more durable and precise compared to those from an inkjet printer. Furthermore, the precision and speed of laser printers, along with the robustness of the toner, make this setup especially suitable for creating high-quality decals that enhance the longevity and aesthetic appeal of scale models. Therefore, for modelers prioritizing a straightforward printing process and long-lasting results, opting for a laser printer and corresponding laser decal paper is the optimal choice.

Decal Paper and Printer Settings: Once you've chosen your decal paper, adjust your printer settings to achieve the highest quality print as recommended by the decal paper manufacturer. This typically means setting your printer to a high-resolution photo setting, which helps capture all the intricate details of your decal design accurately. Note that if you are placing instruments onto a dark surface, you will need "white" decal paper as this provides a white carrier film for the decals. The only drawback is that the decals will need to be cut precisely around the image so that none of the white carrier film shows.

Printing: Before printing your decals on the actual decal paper, it is advisable to print a test page on regular paper. This step allows you to check for color accuracy and size correctness, ensuring that your decals will look exactly as intended when transferred to the model. After making any necessary adjustments and ensuring you are satisfied with the test print, proceed to print the decals on the decal paper.

Applying Decals

Applying decals to the cockpit of a scale model is a delicate process that requires careful preparation and execution to ensure the decals adhere smoothly and appear seamless once applied.

Surface Preparation: Start by ensuring the area where the decals will be applied is thoroughly clean and free from any debris. This ensures that no particles interfere with the adhesion process. Additionally, the panel should be completely painted prior to the decal application as this should be the very last step.

Decal Application: Once the surface is prepared and the decals are printed, carefully cut out the decals from the sheet (using various sizes of sharpened brass tubes can be used to cut out individual circular dials). Soak them in water as per the instructions provided with the decal paper. This soaking loosens the decal from the backing paper, facilitating easier handling and positioning on the model. Gently position the decals on the model using a soft brush, which assists in placing the decals accurately and smoothing out any air bubbles or excess water. During this phase, incorporating products like Micro Set can be very beneficial. Be gentle during this process to avoid tearing the delicate decals.

Enhancing Decal Adhesion and Conformity: For decals that need to conform to textured surfaces or complex curves, applying Micro Sol after positioning the decal can be advantageous. Micro Sol is a solution that softens decals further, making them more pliable and allowing them to stretch into crevices and around protrusions, which enhances the realism of the application.

Sealing: After the decals have been positioned correctly and are completely dry, you can optionally apply a clear coat over them. This sealing protects the decals from peeling or damage from handling and environmental factors. Furthermore, the clear coat aids in visually integrating the decals into the cockpit, giving them an appearance that mimics part of the original paint job. This not only protects your work but also elevates the overall realism of the model, making the decals look as though they were originally part of the aircraft's design.

Functional Lighting and Displays

Adding functional lighting and displays can dramatically enhance the realism of a cockpit in scale models, bringing it to life with dynamic and visually appealing features. This section offers a basic introduction to incorporating electrical components into your model, highlighting options for those interested in exploring these advanced enhancements.

Integrating Lighting: Integrating lighting into your model involves careful planning and precise execution. This includes laying out where each light will enhance the model most effectively, such as in instrument panels, gauges, or other displays. The installation often requires drilling tiny holes to fit the lights and routing wires discreetly to maintain the aesthetic integrity of the cockpit. The discreet routing of wires is crucial for keeping the interior looking clean and realistic, as visible wires can detract from the scale realism. When selecting LEDs, it's important to choose components that match the scale and intensity required for your model, considering the size and luminosity. Information on voltage requirements is crucial as it ensures the longevity and safety of the installation. Safe wiring practices are essential to prevent any electrical mishaps and ensure that the lights function correctly within the model.

Third-Party MFDs and HUDs: For those looking to incorporate more complex features, third-party Multi-Function Displays (MFDs) and Heads-Up Displays (HUDs) offer advanced options. These can be seamlessly integrated into panels and consoles, providing an additional layer of realism and functionality. This is especially the case when designing your own panels as the panels can be designed around the desired displays. For enthusiasts aiming to add sophisticated and interactive elements to their scale models, third-party Multi-Function Displays (MFDs) and Heads-Up Displays (HUDs) present compelling advanced options. Many third-party companies offer a range of these high-quality, ready-to-install components, providing a variety of choices to fit different model specifications and personal preferences. These products are excellent for those looking to elevate their models cockpit with dynamic, realistic cockpit interfaces.

Powering Your Setup: Powering the electrical components effectively and discreetly is the final step. Various battery options are available, which can be chosen based on the power needs and space constraints of your model. Ideally, the power is integrated as a part of the receiver power so that a separate battery isn't necessary.

Incorporating these electrical components not only adds a significant visual appeal but also brings a new level of interaction and realism to your scale modeling projects. While third-party solutions provide an easier route for those less inclined to DIY, the satisfaction of customizing and integrating these systems on your own can greatly enhance the personal value and uniqueness of your model.

Bridging Technology and Realism

In this chapter, we have explored the sophisticated techniques of high-fidelity customization through 3D printing, the meticulous application of decals, and the strategic integration of functional lighting and displays. The next chapter shifts our attention to the art of creating realistic pilot figures that embody the spirit and precision of your detailed cockpits. Here, we will explore customization and even animation to ensure that your pilots are as dynamic and engaging as the cockpits they inhabit. This natural progression from static cockpit elements to dynamic human figures will enhance the realism of your models, making each display or flight an immersive experience.

Chapter 5: Pilot Detailing, Painting and Animation

The realism of a model is often measured not just by the accuracy of its structure and paint, but also by the life it seems to embody. This is where pilot figures come into play, serving as pivotal elements that breathe life into an RC model. Pilot figures do more than fill a seat; they add a layer of depth and realism that connects the model to its real-world counterpart. By detailing and animating these figures, modelers can elevate the authenticity of their creations, making each aircraft a snapshot of a moment in aviation history.

The integration of detailed pilots into accurately recreated cockpits results in a powerful synergy that enhances the overall impact of the model. This chapter will explore how the detailed cockpits designed in previous chapters can be complemented by their animated inhabitants. Through detailed painting, character enhancement, and dynamic animation, these figures can reflect the operation and era of the aircraft, adding an essential element of realism that static models lack. The aim is to not only capture the appearance of a pilot but to evoke the essence of their interaction with the aircraft, whether it's a calm reconnaissance flight or a high-stakes combat mission. This holistic approach to modeling ensures that every component, from the instrument panels to the pilot's expression, tells a cohesive and compelling story.

Choosing the right scale for your pilot is essential to maintaining realism. A pilot being too large or too small can result in a toyish look.

Choosing the Right Scale Pilot Figure

The first step is selecting the appropriate figure that matches the scale and style of your aircraft. It's crucial to choose a figure that not only fits physically within the cockpit but also accurately represents the era and type of the aircraft. For example, a World War II fighter would require a pilot with appropriate historical gear and attire, while a modern jet fighter would need a pilot with a contemporary flight suit and helmet.

You can find a selection of high-quality pilot figures tailored to different types of aircraft on my website, thercgeek.com/pilots. Each figure is 3D Printed in fine detail and comes in various styles to match many aircraft eras and types, ensuring that you can find the perfect pilot to complement your model.

How to Select the Right Pilot Scale

The scale of a model aircraft tells you how much smaller the model is compared to the real aircraft. It is typically expressed as a ratio, such as 1:12, which means the model is 1/12th the size of the actual aircraft.

If you don't already know the scale of your model (often times it's not listed), you can measure it and compare it to the known dimensions of the full-scale aircraft. You can find the dimensions of most full scale aircraft online with a quick search. Common measurements include the wingspan, so take a measurement of the model wingspan and then find this measurement for the full scale aircraft.

Once you have both measurements, calculate the scale by using the formula:

$$Scale = \frac{Full\ Scale\ Aircraft\ Dimension}{Model\ Dimension}$$

For example, if the full scale aircraft has a wingspan of 40 feet (480 inches) and your model has a wingspan of 48 inches, the scale would be:

$$Scale = \frac{480\ inches}{48\ inches} = 10$$

This means your model is 1:10 scale.

Once you know the scale of your model, choosing a pilot figure is simple as pilot figures are typically labeled with their scale (e.g., 1:10 or 1/10 scale) to help you match them to your model.

Painting and Detailing Pilot Figures

Building on the foundational skills covered in Chapter 3 where we discussed how to paint and select the proper scale pilot, this section delves deeper into the specialized techniques of painting and detailing pilot figures to enhance their realism and integration into the cockpit environment. Choosing the right materials and employing meticulous painting techniques are crucial steps in bringing a pilot figure to life.

Materials and Paint Types

Selecting the appropriate paints is paramount for achieving optimal results in detailing pilot figures. When it comes to painting these intricate components, the choice of paint can greatly influence the final appearance and durability of your models.

Enamel Paints for Base and Detail Work: Enamel paints are favored for their exceptional durability and vibrant color quality, making them excellent for the base coating and fine detailing of pilot figures. These paints provide a smooth, hard finish that is less prone to chipping, which is ideal for figures that may be handled frequently. Enamels also offer fine pigmentation, which is crucial for capturing the minute details of military uniforms, flight suits, and historical attire accurately. However, enamel paints require more careful handling due to their longer drying times and the need for solvents for cleanup.

Acrylic Paints/Pigments for Washes and Additional Effects: Acrylic paints, known for their ease of use and quick drying times, are highly recommended for adding washes and other effects to enhance the depth and texture of the pilot figures. Their water solubility allows for easy mixing and cleanup, making them ideal for applying subtle shading and highlighting effects after the enamel base has dried. Acrylics can be diluted to create washes that settle into the crevices of the figure, accentuating details such as facial features and fabric folds. This combination of enamel for the foundational layers and acrylics for detailed effects allows modelers to leverage the strengths of both types of paints to produce a highly detailed and durable finish.

By understanding the properties and applications of both enamel and acrylic paints, modelers can effectively choose the right materials for each stage of the painting process, ensuring that their pilot figures are not only visually striking but also built to last.

Pilot Figure Painting Techniques

Painting pilot figures requires a methodical approach to ensure that they authentically complement the detailed scale model aircraft they inhabit. The process begins with the first step of applying a base coat, followed by the application of the base color, which sets the visual tone for the figure.

Once the foundation is set, we move into the task of adding details—facial features, uniform specifics, and insignias—that bring the figure to life. This phase demands precision and a steady hand to capture the subtle nuances that define a pilot's character. Lastly, the techniques of shading and highlighting are discussed to add depth and texture, transforming a two-dimensional appearance into a three-dimensional figure brimming with realism. Each step, from base coating to detailed finishing touches, is essential for achieving a professional and lifelike result that enhances the overall presentation of your scale model.

The base colors of white (helmet) and green (flight suit) are in place on this pilot bust.

Detail painting is underway with the floatation gear and oxygen mask painted Olive Drab.

Base Coating: The first step in painting a pilot figure involves applying a primer. Primer serves as a foundation that enhances the adhesion of subsequent paint layers and increases the durability of the paint job. Once the primer has set, apply a uniform base coat. This layer establishes the predominant color of the figure's outfit and should be applied evenly ideally being sprayed with an airbrush or spray can.Ensure that the base coat is completely dry before moving on to more detailed painting to prevent smudging and blending of colors.

Detail Painting: With the base coat in place, the next step focuses on adding intricate details such as belt straps, uniform specifics, and insignias. Using fine brushes, carefully paint the smaller details with their appropriate colors ensuring full and complete coverage into the corners and recesses. For facial features, subtle color variations can be used to mimic skin tones and details like eyes and lips. Uniform details such as buttons, belts, and patches require steady hands and a bit of patience to accurately depict. Again, use the appropriate colors to paint each of the desired details. Insignias and patches can either be hand-painted or applied using tiny decals if available.

With all of the detail painting complete, the bust is then sprayed with a matte clear.

The final touch is the paint the visor with gloss gun metal metallic to give it a high shine and luminescent sheen.

The final painted pilot compared to the included stock pilot that came with the kit. The difference in realism is substantial.

Shading and Highlighting: To bring out the depth and texture of the pilot's attire and features, shading and highlighting techniques are essential. Washes are particularly effective for shading; which involve applying a diluted darker acrylic paint into the recesses of the figure, which enhances depth and accentuates the details. Dry brushing, on the other hand, is used for highlighting raised features. This technique involves lightly brushing a lighter color over the raised surfaces of the figure, which helps to create a sense of volume and realism by simulating light reflection. Both techniques are pivotal in adding depth; however, if you must choose one, dry brushing is recommended for its simplicity and effectiveness.

Clear Coating: After completing the painting and detailing, apply a matte clear coat to protect your work and enhance the durability of the paint job. This step not only seals in the colors and details but also provides a uniform sheen that contributes to the overall visual appeal of the figure.

Glossy Visors & Goggles: To obtain an effective look on visors and goggles, these can either be painted with gloss paints after the clear coat has been applied and/or apply a high-gloss clear coat only to these specific areas. This technique will mimic the reflective properties of glass and add another layer of realism to your pilot figures. Careful application is key to ensure the gloss enhances these features without affecting the surrounding areas.

Animating Pilot Figures

Animating pilot figures brings an unmatched level of realism and engagement to scale models, transforming an otherwise static area into dynamic representations of real-life scenarios. This process involves integrating servo mechanisms into the pilot figures to enable controlled, realistic movements such as head turning or limb articulation.

The first step in animating a pilot figure is selecting the right servo. The size and type of servo are dictated by the scale of the model and the specific movements required. Micro servos are generally ideal for most applications because they offer sufficient torque for moving light parts like a pilot's head while maintaining a compact size and light weight that can be easily concealed within the figure.

To prepare for servo installation, begin by modifying the pilot figure to accommodate the servo. This begins by first removing the part from the pilot figure (if needed) while attachment of any necessary detail parts (again, if needed). This can be accomplished by the use of a razor saw. From there, using a Dremel tool with a router bit, carefully remove the back portion of the figure where the servo will be placed. It's essential to perform this step with precision to avoid overcutting areas and damaging the figure's aesthetics or structural integrity. Once the space is prepared, test fit the servo to ensure it fits in perfect alignment to the hole where the articulated part would be (neck for head, shoulder for arm, etc.). Once satisfied, the servo can be secured with hot glue, ensuring it is firmly mounted and correctly aligned for the desired movement.

A carbon tube and servo arm will double as the head and servo attachment.

With the back opened up with a Dremel, a micro servo gets glued into the pilot and later covered again.

It's important to ensure that the servo and neck attachment align well within the pilot body to avoid binding and inadvertently popping off.

Attaching the pilot's head or whichever element to be animated involves connecting it to the servo. This is typically done by affixing a carbon rod or tube to the center of the servo arm, then attaching the other end of the rod to the head or part that is to be animated. It's crucial to test the setup manually to ensure smooth movement without any binding. Additionally, this realistically should be done in combination with gluing the servo in place to ensure that the alignment is perfect. Also, take care in making sure that the carbon rod length and placement are correct before final gluing any parts or pieces.

The wiring for the servo is that strategically routed to remain hidden which is typically down through the seat area to preserve the clean look of the model. Ideal concealment paths include through the pilot seat out to the outer floor of the cockpit or within the aircraft's body, using small gauge wires to reduce visibility and interference if needed.

Finally, the servo is ideally connected to a control system capable of generating random and independent movements, such as a Random Servo Motion Generator available from www.thercgeek.com/RSMG. This system allows for the programming of realistic and seemingly spontaneous movements for up to two servos. Adjusting the range and speed of the servo's motion is key to achieving lifelike actions that enhance rather than detract from the model's realism.

By carefully planning the integration of servos and ensuring complete execution of each step—from the initial modifications to the final programming—animating pilot figures can be done relatively simply. This addition not only enhances the visual appeal of the models but also enriches the storytelling aspect, making each model not just a static display but a vivid scene captured in motion. This subtle feature makes a tremendous impact, bringing scale models to life with realistic action.

It is worth noting that if you're looking to outfit a larger airframe with a moving pilot, warbirdpilots.com offers pilot figures with pre-installed servos for moving heads from about 1/7 scale up to 1/4 scale and larger.

Expanding Horizons: Beyond Basic Pilot Detailing

As we wrap up this chapter on the detailed painting and animation of pilot figures, consider this the beginning of a broader adventure in cockpit detailing. The skills and methods we've explored are not just steps to improve your pilot figures but can be considered pathways to greater artistic expression within the hobby.

I encourage you to experiment with the techniques we've discussed. Whether refining your painting skills, experimenting with different texturing effects, or integrating simple animations, each new technique you master can transform your models and enhance your enjoyment.

Continue to push the boundaries of what you can achieve with your scale models. Experiment with new materials, adopt innovative techniques, and look for ways to add a personal touch to your work. Remember, each model is a canvas for your creativity and a chance to express your passion for the art of scale modeling. Keep building, keep learning, and most importantly, enjoy the process of bringing your imaginative visions to life.

Just as with anything in this hobby, building a cockpit can involve as much or as little detail as you desire. Ultimately, it's about artistic expression and discovering joy in the journey.

Chapter 6: Case Studies in Scale Cockpit Customization

This chapter provides detailed case studies of specific projects that illustrate the transformation of standard model interiors into detailed masterpieces. By exploring the modifications and techniques applied in these examples, you can gain insights into how various methods and materials can be utilized to enhance scale models significantly. We'll focus on three projects: a refinished Freewing F-14 Tomcat and a competition scale Jet Hangar Hobbies A-7 Corsair II, and a scratch-built F4D Skyray, each showcasing a unique approach to interior creation and customization.

F-14 Tomcat: Integration of 3D Printed Parts and Custom Decals

The Freewing F-14 Tomcat project exemplifies the use of advanced 3D printing technology and custom decals to upgrade a model's interior. This interior was transformed using almost exclusively 3D printed parts to replace and enhance the cockpit details, which were originally basic foam parts that lacked any realism.

Design and Printing of 3D Parts: For the F-14 Tomcat, the entire cockpit was assessed for areas that could benefit from enhanced realism. Key components such as the instrument panels and ejection seats were designed using CAD software, carefully ensuring that each part would fit precisely within the existing cockpit space. The parts were printed using a high-resolution resin printer, chosen for its ability to capture fine details essential for the cockpit's small scale. Once printed, the parts were cleaned and painted using the processes described previously.

Custom Decals for Gauges: To complement the 3D printed parts, custom decals were created for all gauges and displays. Images found online of the F-14's cockpit panels were sourced, then adjusted in graphic design software to fit the scale. They were also used in the design process as the base by which the instrument panels were designed around. Decals were printed on white laser jet decal paper, which ensured sharp details and color fidelity. The decals were cut exactly to shape and then applied meticulously to the 3D printed panels, providing a level of detail that painted gauges could not achieve.

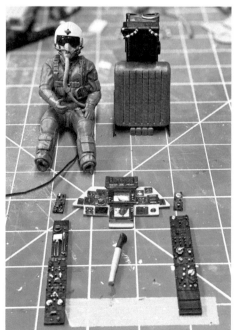

The painted, weathered, and ready to install front cockpit parts & pilot.

Pilot Figure Detailing: Equally detailed pilot figures were 3D printed and added to enhance the cockpit's realism further. The figure was carefully scaled to match the scale and era of the aircraft and a servo added into each to animate the heads. Detailed painting techniques including shading, and highlighting, were used to bring the pilots to life, emphasizing the uniform's textures and features.

Final Assembly and Detailing: Once all parts were printed, painted, and the decals applied, the components were assembled within the cockpit. Special attention was paid to the alignment and positioning, ensuring that each piece meshed well with its surroundings. Additional weathering techniques were applied to give a used and operational look to the cockpit, enhancing the realism further.

The finished cockpit in the F-14 Tomcat prior to gluing the canopy in place.

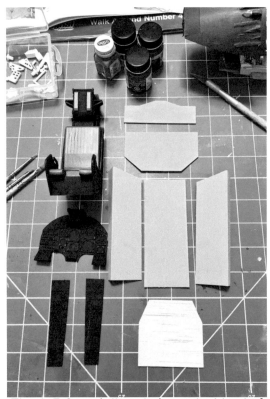

The A-7 Corsair II cockpit used a blend of balsawood & 3D printed parts.

A-7 Corsair II: Combining Scratch-Built Elements with 3D Printed Technology

The Jet Hangar Hobbies A-7 Corsair II project showcases a hybrid approach, combining traditional scratch-built techniques with selective 3D printing to enhance the model's fidelity.

Scratch-Built Elements: Traditional modeling techniques were employed to craft specific elements of the A-7 Corsair II's cockpit such as the cockpit tub and instrument panels and consoles. Using materials such as styrene sheets and balsa wood, the larger cockpit structures were hand-crafted. From there, the instrument panels and side consoles were created from a silicone mold resulting from scratch built panels that had been built years prior. These elements were detailed with switches and dial openings and then molded for replication.

3D Printed Ejection Seat: To upgrade the pilot's SJU-8 ejection seat, a detailed 3D model was designed and printed. The seat was enhanced with all of the desired elements in the CAD modeling process to allow for detailed painting during assembly. This approach allowed for a more detailed and realistic ejection seat compared to what could be achieved through traditional modeling alone.

Pilot Figure Integration and Customization: A commercially available pilot figure was integrated into the cockpit to complement the detailed ejection seat. The figure was custom-painted with particular attention to the pilot's suit and gear to add a personal touch to the final product.

Integration and Detailing: The scratch-built elements and 3D printed seat were integrated into the cockpit, with careful attention to how these different techniques complemented each other. Painting and weathering tied all elements together, providing a cohesive and detailed appearance. The final result was a highly realistic cockpit that retained the hand-crafted charm of traditional models while incorporating the precision of modern 3D printing.

The completed A-7 Corsair II cockpit both in and out of the model. The map pockets on the instrument panel hood were simply made from masking tape.

Scratch-Built F4D Skyray: Custom Cockpit and Pilot Integration

The scratch-built F4D Skyray project demonstrates a tailored approach to cockpit enhancement using a mix of scratch-building and 3D printing techniques focused on a half cockpit setup.

Cockpit Design and 3D Printing: The F4D Skyray's cockpit, particularly the seat and instrument panel hood, was designed and 3D printed to fit precisely within the existing model structure. The half cockpit design was optimized for visibility and integration with the model's scale and detailing requirements. It should be noted that these elements could have just as easily been scratch built from depron or balsawood.

Instrument Panel Creation: Instead of using individual instruments, the instrument panel face was created by scaling an accurate image of the F4D's cockpit, which was then attached using spray adhesive to the 3D printed panel. This method provided a quick and effective solution to detailing the panel while maintaining a high level of realism.

Pilot Bust Customization: A pilot bust was scaled and 3D printed to match the cockpit's dimensions. It was then detailed with the painting techniques we've discussed to bring the pilot to life within the limited visible area of the half cockpit.

Final Assembly and Integration: The cockpit components were carefully assembled, ensuring that the integration of the printed elements and the pilot bust created a seamless appearance. The focus was on making sure that the visible parts of the cockpit were as detailed and realistic as possible, enhancing the overall aesthetic of the Skyray model.

Not all cockpits have to be full depth. A half cockpit like in this F4D Skyray is very effective.

Legend Hobby A-1 Skyraider: Enhancing a Stock Cockpit with Simple Techniques and a Movable Pilot

The A-1 Skyraider by Legend Hobby serves as a superb example of how a stock cockpit can be transformed with minimal but effective enhancements. Initially, the cockpit setup was constructed straight from the kit (they provide a great assortment of cockpit parts in the kit), which provided a solid foundation but lacked personalized details that could elevate its realism.

Simple Dry Brushing Technique: To enhance the stock cockpit, a simple dry brushing technique was employed. Using a silver color, dry brushing was applied strategically across the cockpit's raised details. This approach highlighted the textures and features, giving depth and a worn look that closely mimics the operational wear seen in the full scale aircraft.

Incorporating a Movable Pilot Figure: A significant addition to the cockpit was the integration of a movable 1/7 scale pilot figure sourced from warbirdpilots.com. This pilot, designed to fit perfectly within the A-1's cockpit, was not only proportionally accurate but also featured a moving servo operated head that allowed for dynamic realism. The figure's inclusion significantly boosted the authenticity of the model, making it not just a static display but a snapshot of a live cockpit scenario.

With the movable pilot in the A-1 Skyraider, the finished cockpit becomes a much more dynamic feature on the model.

Outcome and Reflections: The enhancements made to the A-1 Skyraider's cockpit, though straightforward, had a profound impact on the model's overall authenticity and appeal. Simple techniques like dry brushing brought out the finer details of the cockpit, while the addition of a movable pilot added a layer of realism that can be appreciated in both static displays and during flight. This case study underscores the value of even the smallest modifications and how they can transform a stock model into a standout piece on any flight line or display shelf.

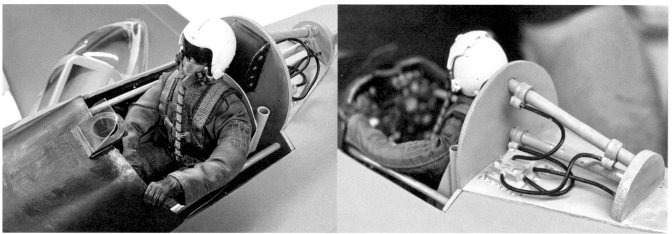

Through some simple paint work and a commercially available pilot, the A-1 Skyraider cockpit came to life.

These case studies demonstrate the rich variety of methods and approaches available for creating detailed and realistic scale aircraft interiors. Whether you leverage the precision of advanced 3D printing, embrace the craftsmanship of traditional scratch-building, or innovate with new materials, the possibilities to enhance your models are boundless. Don't hesitate to experiment with different techniques; you might discover that they are more approachable than they initially seem. Remember, while 3D printing offers cutting-edge possibilities, traditional scratch-building remains a deeply rewarding and often quicker alternative for adding unique touches to your cockpits. Each project offers a chance to expand your skills, express your creativity, and achieve personal satisfaction in bringing your projects vision to life.

A detailed cockpit combined with an authentically painted and weathered finish will completely transform any scale RC model, as showcased by this custom-painted A-1 Skyraider soaring through the skies.

Chapter 7: Embracing the Journey

As we close this book on elevating the artistry of scale aircraft interiors, it's important to reflect not just on the specific techniques and projects discussed, but on the broader journey of learning and growth that modeling offers. Aim for continued experimentation and understand the importance of community in this rewarding hobby. It's a celebration of where we've been and an invitation to where we can go next.

The Path of Continual Learning and Experimentation

Each project presents a unique set of challenges and opportunities to push the boundaries of what you can create. The techniques covered in this book—from basic painting and detailing to advanced 3D printing and pilot animation—are just starting points. The true depth of your skills will be honed through continual practice and experimentation.

Embrace the process of learning as much as the final outcome. Each model you build is not just an end product but a step in your ongoing development as a modeler. Try new materials, adapt the techniques you've learned, and don't be afraid to make mistakes. Sometimes, the best learning experiences come from projects that don't go as planned, providing valuable lessons that can be applied to future endeavors.

Sharing Your Work and Learning from the Community

Scale modeling is not just a solitary activity; it thrives on the shared passion and collective wisdom of its community. Engaging with other modelers can significantly enhance your experience and skill set.

Showcasing Your Work: Sharing your completed projects can be incredibly rewarding. Whether through social media, modeling forums, or local clubs, showcasing your work invites feedback that can inspire and challenge you to improve. I t also allows you to celebrate your achievements and journey, contributing to your sense of accomplishment and motivation.

Learning from Others: The scale modeling community is remarkably collaborative. Many modelers enjoy sharing their techniques and solutions to common problems. Participate in forums, attend workshops, and connect with other enthusiasts at shows or competitions. Watching others work and discussing different approaches can open your eyes to methods and ideas that you might not have considered.

Contributing to the Community: As you grow in your skills and knowledge, consider giving back to the community that supports you. Sharing your knowledge not only helps others but also solidifies your own understanding and appreciation of the craft. For those looking to delve even deeper, consider exploring the additional resources and community support offered through www.thercgeek.com. Here, you'll find a platform for further learning, sharing, and even membership options to enhance your modeling journey.

Looking Forward

As this book concludes, consider how far you have come and how much further you can go in the world of scale modeling. The skills you've developed and the knowledge you've gained form a foundation upon which you can build increasingly complex and rewarding projects. Look forward with enthusiasm to your next model, ready to apply all that you've learned and eager to discover even more.

Keep experimenting, keep learning, and keep sharing. Your journey in scale modeling is as much about the community and continuous growth as it is about each individual project. Remember, every modeler was once a beginner, and every expert has a story of a project that taught them something new. Your journey in scale modeling is a perpetual flight towards greater skill and deeper satisfaction—enjoy every part of the ride.

Holding my partially painted, scratch-built F4D Skyray, I'm reminded of the journey each model represents. Dive into your next project with enthusiasm, and remember—every model is a canvas for your creativity and passion.

Bonus: Creating Unique Details with Everyday Materials

In the realm of scale modeling, resourcefulness transforms everyday materials into spectacular details that enhance the realism of any project. This chapter celebrates the inventive spirit of modelers who look beyond traditional modeling supplies to create unique cockpit accents. Crafting items from simple materials like masking tape and a Sharpie exemplifies how ordinary items can be reimagined into intricate components of a scale model's interior. Such techniques not only add a layer of authenticity to the model but also infuse a sense of personal artistry and innovation into the build. Embracing this approach can unlock new creative possibilities, making each project not just a display of skill but also a testament to imaginative resourcefulness.

Crafting Simple Map Pouches and Pockets Using Masking Tape

In scale modeling, it's often the smallest details that bring a cockpit to life, transforming a good model into a great one. This bonus section introduces a simple, innovative technique to add realistic map pouches and pockets to your aircraft's cockpit using everyday materials like masking window, a black Sharpie, and a small piece of wire. This approach not only enhances the authenticity of the cockpit but also adds a personal touch that sets your model apart.

From simple masking tape and a Sharpie to a detailed cockpit pouch.

Materials and Preparation: Start with a piece of masking tape, cutting it to the desired size based on the scale of your model and the intended prominence of the pouch. Use a black Sharpie to color one side of the masking tape, which will mimic the fabric of the map pouch and give it a distinct, worn look.

Adding Structure: Cut a smaller strip of tape, about one-third the width of your main piece, and lay a thin, flexible, yet sturdy wire along its center. This wire will help maintain the shape of the pouch and add some rigidity. Carefully fold your larger, colored tape over this wire, ensuring the wire is centered and the colored side is outward. Press firmly to make sure the tape sticks to itself, encapsulating the wire.

Forming the Pouch: Once your tape is sealed around the wire, gently scrunch the assembly to create the appearance of an elastic band or a gathered fabric effect. This simulates the realistic look of a pouch that could expand and contract, as seen in actual cockpit storage solutions.

The final pouch shows how everyday materials can be artfully transformed into essential cockpit details.

Installation: Position the finished tape pouch in your cockpit at the desired location. The wire's flexibility allows you to adjust the pouch's shape to fit snugly against other cockpit elements or within confined spaces. If necessary, a small dab of glue can be used to secure the pouch in place, or it can be left unattached for adjustability and removable during future modifications.

This straightforward technique is an excellent example of how everyday materials can be repurposed to add significant detail and personality to scale models. So, I encourage you to think creatively and use simple tools to enhance the realism and individuality of your projects. By integrating such custom details, you not only improve the visual appeal of your model but also engage more deeply with the craft, enjoying each step of the creative process.

Unlock Even More with Exclusive Resources!

Elevate Your Skills with the Masterclass Video

Dive deeper into the art of cockpit detailing with the exclusive cockpit painting Masterclass Video Series. Perfectly complementing the techniques and projects discussed in this book, this video offers detailed tutorials that bring the lessons to life. Visit www.artofscalemodeling.com/cockpit to access the video exclusively for readers. Enhance your modeling skills with expert guidance and step-by-step demonstrations that make complex techniques easy to understand and apply.

Discover the Comprehensive Guide on Scale Aircraft Painting & Finishing

If you enjoyed this journey through cockpit detailing, don't miss out on the comprehensive guide to scale aircraft painting and finishing. "Mastering the Art of Scale Aircraft Painting & Finishing" is available at www.artofscalemodeling.com. This book & Masterclass video series is a must-have for anyone looking to perfect their painting techniques and add a professional finish to their models. Explore a wealth of knowledge through the 5-step method that has led to two US Scale National Championships.

Both resources are designed to help you transform your scale models from the ordinary to the extraordinary. Whether you're a seasoned modeler or just starting out, these tools will enhance your capabilities and inspire you to create more intricate and realistic models.

Visit today and start your next project with confidence!

Chris Wolfe

Made in the USA
Columbia, SC
09 September 2024

41343806R00029